D0744521

The SAINTS

SPEAK TO YOU

TODAY

The SAINTS SPEAK TO YOU TODAY

365 DAILY REMINDERS

COLLECTED AND WITH AN INTRODUCTION
BY MITCH FINLEY

CHARIS

SERVANT PUBLICATIONS
ANN ARBOR, MICHIGAN

Charis Books is an imprint of Servant Publications especially designed to serve
Roman Catholics.

Servant Publications
P.O. Box 8617
Ann Arbor, MI 48107

Cover design: Left Coast Design, Portland, Oregon
Cover illustration: Mary, Queen of Heaven, National Gallery of Art, Washington
D.C./Superstock, Inc. Used by permission.

99 00 01 02 10 9 8 7 6 5 4 3 2 1

Printed in the United States of America
ISBN 1-56955-141-3

LIBRARY OF CONGRESS CATALOGING-IN-PUBLICATION DATA

The saints speak to you today : 365 daily reminders / collected and with an introduction by Mitch Finley.
    p.   cm.
  ISBN 1-56955-141-3 (alk. paper)
  1. Meditations. 2. Spiritual life—Catholic Church. 3. Devotional calendars—
Catholic Church. I. Finley, Mitch.
BX2178.S25   1999
242'.2—dc21   99-22970
                                                  CIP

INTRODUCTION

Countless people are hungry for spiritual wisdom today, and the saints are spiritual experts. They are authorities on the wisdom of the heart and the wisdom of the spirit. Because they experienced a special closeness with God in this world, their words are both lighter and heavier than the words of the average person. Their words are lighter because they communicate the freedom and joy of heaven. Their words are heavier because they speak with special insight of the things that matter most in this life.

The saints whose words fill this book lived in many times and places, from the earliest days of the Christian community right up to the twentieth century. They lived their faith in their own time and place, but their spiritual wisdom is a wisdom for all times, all places, and all seasons. The saints speak to the human heart because the heart of a saint is filled with the love of God, the God who—as St. Augustine of Hippo (354–430) said—is closer to us than we are to ourselves.

Each of the saints was a unique human being, with his or her unique ideals and idiosyncracies. Some had a solemn outlook on life, while others were as lighthearted as an angel. The saints varied from holy bums like St. Joseph Benedict Labré (1748–83) and simple peasants like St. Bernadette Soubirous (1844–79) to theological geniuses like St. Thomas Aquinas (c. 1225–74) and heroic martyrs like St. Maximilian Kolbe (1894–1941). Yet all, to a one, lived a life dedicated to love of God and neighbor.

By their lives and by their words the saints shed light on the world's dark places. When our own lives are painful or difficult, when meaning seems to escape our grasp, the saints remind us that—in words from a song by singer-songwriter John Stewart—"when things go wrong they happen for the best." The saints remind us of the basics: faith, hope, and love. They remind us of the importance of simple prayer, trust in God's love, and belief in the ultimate goodness of life. They remind us that our days are always worth living, and they remind us that God's love for us has no limits.

The holy men and women quoted in this book fall into two classifications. Some saints are officially canonized. Their names have been enrolled on the Roman Catholic church's calendar—a list of those determined, as far as humanly possible, to be eternally united to Christ in heaven. Those called "blessed" are one step away from canonization—that is, from being included on the official list of saints, those declared to be, without a doubt, in heaven and worthy of public honor. Both the saints and those who are "blessed" qualify as guides in this life. They offer wisdom and inspiration, and they are heavenly friends and companions on our pilgrimage in this world. Let their words lift you up, one day at a time.

Mitch Finley
Feast of All Saints,
November 1, 1998

1

In God alone is there primordial and true delight, and in all our delights it is this delight that we are seeking.

ST. BONAVENTURE (13TH C.)

2

After I enter the chapel I place myself in the presence of God and I say to him, "Lord, here I am; give me whatever you wish." If he gives me something, then I am happy and I thank him. If he does not give me anything then I thank him nonetheless, knowing, as I do, that I deserve nothing. Then I begin to tell him of all that concerns me, my joys, my thoughts, my distress, and finally, I listen to him.

ST. CATHERINE LABOURÉ (19TH C.)

3

O how glorious our faith is! Instead of restricting hearts, as the world fancies, it uplifts them and enlarges their capacity to love, to love with an almost infinite love, since it will continue unbroken beyond our mortal life.

ST. THÉRÈSE OF LISIEUX (19TH C.)

4

I saw that [God] is everything that is good and comfortable for us. He is our clothing. In his love he wraps and holds us. He enfolds us for love, and he will never let us go.

BL. JULIAN OF NORWICH (15TH C.)

5

St. Francis de Sales, that great saint, would leave off writing with the
letter of a word half-formed in order to reply to an interruption.

ST. JOHN VIANNEY (19TH C.)

6

My Good Shepherd, who have shown your very gentle mercy to us
unworthy sinners in various physical pains and sufferings, give grace
and strength to me, your little lamb, that in no tribulation or anguish
or pain may I turn away from you.

ST. FRANCIS OF ASSISI (13TH C.)

7

If you ate only one meal a week would you survive? It is the same for your soul. Nourish it with the Blessed Sacrament.

BL. ANDRÉ BESSETTE (20TH C.)

8

The parting of the ways occurs right at the Child's manger; even there, he is King of Kings and Lord of Lords. "Follow me," he commands, and anyone who is not for him is against him. We too are confronted with these words, and the decision they pose between light and darkness.

ST. EDITH STEIN (20TH C.)

9

I pray God may open your eyes and let you see what hidden treasures he bestows on us in the trials from which the world thinks only to flee.

ST. JOHN OF AVILA (16TH C.)

10

The Christian who desires to follow Jesus carrying his cross must bear in mind that the name "Christian" means "learner or imitator of Christ" and that if he wishes to bear that noble title worthily he must above all do as Christ charges us in the gospel; we must oppose or deny ourselves, take up the cross, and follow him.

ST. ANTHONY MARY CLARET (19TH C.)

11

Do something good for someone you like least, today.

ST. ANTHONY OF PADUA (13TH C.)

12

Just as every sort of gem when cast in honey becomes brighter and
more sparkling, so each person becomes more acceptable and fitting in
his own vocation when he sets that vocation in the context of devotion. Through devotion family cares become more peaceful, mutual
love between husband and wife becomes more sincere ... and our
work, no matter what it is, becomes more pleasant and agreeable.

ST. FRANCIS DE SALES (16TH C.)

13

My religion teaches me to pardon my enemies and all who have offended me. I do gladly pardon the emperor and all who have sought my death. I beg them to seek baptism and be Christians themselves.

ST. PAUL MIKI (16TH C.)

14

A Christian has a union with Jesus Christ more noble, more intimate and more perfect than the members of a human body have with their head. He longs to be in you, he wants his breath to be your breath, his heart in your heart, and his soul in your soul.

ST. JOHN EUDES (17TH C.)

15

It is right that you should begin again every day. There is no better way to finish the spiritual life than to be ever beginning it over again, and never to think that you have done enough.

ST. FRANCIS DE SALES (17TH C.)

16

One must see God in everyone.

ST. CATHERINE LABOURÉ (19TH C.)

17

O Hope of every contrite heart,

O Joy of all the meek,

To those who fall, how kind You are,

How good to those who seek!

But what to those who find? Ah! This

Nor tongue nor pen can show:

The love of Jesus, what it is

None but his loved ones know.

ST. BERNARD OF CLAIRVAUX (12TH C.)

18

If we look forward to receiving God's mercy, we can never fail to do good as long as we have the strength. For if we share with the poor, out of the love of God, whatever he has given us, we shall receive according to his promise a hundredfold in eternal happiness. What a fine profit, what a blessed reward! Who would not entrust his possessions to this best of merchants who handles our affairs so well.

ST. JOHN OF GOD (16TH C.)

19

Let nothing disturb you,

Let nothing frighten you.

All things are passing.

God alone does not change.

Patience achieves everything.

Whoever has God lacks nothing.

God alone suffices.

St. Teresa of Avila (16th c.)

20

Come, Holy Spirit. Let the precious pearl of the Father and the Word's delight come.

Spirit of truth, You are the reward of the saints, the comforter of souls, light in darkness, riches to the poor, treasure to lovers, food for the hungry, comfort to the wanderer: You are the one in whom all treasures are contained.

ST. MARY MAGDALEN DEI PAZZI (16TH C.)

21

Most high, glorious God, enlighten the darkness of my heart and give me, Lord, a correct faith, a certain hope, a perfect charity, sense, and knowledge, so that I may carry out your holy and true command.

ST. FRANCIS OF ASSISI (13TH C.)

22

Jesus Christ, in his infinite wisdom, used the words and idioms that were in use among those whom he addressed. You should do likewise.

ST. JOSEPH CAFASSO (19TH C.)

23

The heart of a Christian, who believes and feels, cannot pass by the hardships and deprivations of the poor without helping them.

BL. LOUIS GUANELLA (20TH C.)

24

Whoever will proudly dispute and contradict will always stand outside the door. Christ, the master of humility, manifests his truth only to the humble and hides himself from the proud.

ST. VINCENT FERRER (14TH C.)

25

At last I have found my calling! My calling is love!

ST. THÉRÈSE OF LISIEUX (19TH C.)

26

I for the love of Jesus forgive my murderer and I want him to be with me in paradise. May God forgive him, because I have already forgiven him.

ST. MARIA GORETTI (19TH C.)

27

Be eager for more frequent gatherings for thanksgiving to God and his glory, for when you meet thus, the forces of Satan are annulled and his destructive power is canceled in the concord of your faith.

ST. IGNATIUS OF ANTIOCH (2ND C.)

28

Enjoy yourself as much as you like—if only you keep from sin.

ST. JOHN BOSCO (19TH C.)

29

Be merry, really merry. The life of a true Christian should be a perpetual jubilee, a prelude to the festivals of eternity.

BL. THEOPHANE VENARD (19TH C.)

30

Scrupulous souls, forever tormented by doubts and anxiety, have hearts which are ill-prepared to receive Jesus Christ. In place of that peace which religion is meant to give, these souls make their lives miserable, full of trouble and temptation.

BL. HENRY SUSO (14TH C.)

31

To pass judgment on another is to usurp shamelessly a prerogative of God, and to condemn is to ruin one's soul.

ST. JOHN CLIMACUS (7TH C.)

32

Doubtless the state of virginity and continence is more perfect, but this does not prevent marriage from being holy, upright, and perfect in its degree, nor does it prevent those who live in marriage with true fear and love of God from being perfect, upright, and holy.

ST. ANTHONY MARY CLARET (19TH C.)

33

Make many acts of love, for they set the soul on fire and make it gentle. Whatever you do, offer it up to God, and pray it may be for his honor and glory.

ST. TERESA OF AVILA (16TH C.)

34

It is almost certain that excess in eating is the cause of almost all the diseases of the body, but its effects on the soul are even more disastrous.

ST. ALPHONSUS LIGUORI (18TH C.)

35

Every light that comes from Holy Scripture comes from the light of grace. This is why foolish, proud, and learned people are blind even in the light, because the light is clouded by their own pride and selfish love. They read the Scripture literally, not with understanding. They have let go of the light by which the Scripture was formed and proclaimed.

ST. CATHERINE OF SIENA (14TH C.)

36

If knowledge can cause most people to become vain, perhaps ignorance and lack of learning can make them humble. Yet now and then you do find men who pride themselves on their ignorance.

ST. JOHN (7TH C.)

37

My political views are those of the Lord's Prayer.

ST. JOHN BOSCO (19TH C.)

38

I understand now that charity consists in bearing with the faults of others, in not being surprised at their weakness, in being edified by the smallest acts of virtue we see them practice.

ST. THÉRÈSE OF LISIEUX (19TH C.)

39

Learn to fix the eye of faith on the divine word of the Holy Scriptures as on a light shining in a dark place until the day dawn and the daystar arise in our hearts.

ST. AUGUSTINE OF HIPPO (5TH C.)

40

You can advance farther in grace in one hour during a time of affliction than in many days during a time of consolation.

ST. JOHN EUDES (17TH C.)

41

Go and find Jesus when your patience and strength give out and you feel alone and helpless.... Say to him: "Jesus, you know exactly what is going on. You are all I have, and you know all. Come to my help." And then go and don't worry about how you are going to manage. That you have told God about it is enough. He has a good memory.

BL. JEANNE JUGAN (19TH C.)

42

Do not fear what may happen tomorrow. The same loving Father who cares for you today will care for you tomorrow and every day. Either he will shield you from suffering or he will give you unfailing strength to bear it. Be at peace then, and put aside all anxious thoughts and imaginings.

ST. FRANCIS DE SALES (17TH C.)

43

Where there is no love, put love, and you will draw love out.

ST. JOHN OF THE CROSS (16TH C.)

44

The Church was gathered and the faith was believed before ever any part of the New Testament was put in writing.

ST. THOMAS MORE (16TH C.)

45

All this he showed me with great joy, saying, "See, I am God. See, I am in all things. See, I do all things. See, I never take my hands off my work, nor ever shall, through all eternity. See, I lead all things to the end I have prepared for them. I do this through the same wisdom and love and power through which I made them."

BL. JULIAN OF NORWICH (15TH C.)

46

My hope is in God, who has only us with whom to fulfill his plans. It is for us to be faithful and not to spoil his work by our cowardice.

ST. ISAAC JOGUES (17TH C.)

47

Be patient with everyone, but above all with yourself. I mean, do not be disturbed because of your imperfections, and always rise up bravely from a fall.

ST. FRANCIS DE SALES (17TH C.)

48

Death steals on full slyly; unaware
He lies at hand and shall us all surprise,
We know not when nor where nor in what wise.

ST. THOMAS MORE (16TH C.)

49

Our faith is a light, the kindly gift of that endless day which is our
Father, God. By this light our Mother Christ, and our good Lord the
Holy Spirit lead us in this fleeting life.

BL. JULIAN OF NORWICH (15TH C.)

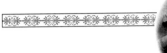

50

For the Christian there is no such thing as a "stranger." There is only the neighbor—the person who happens to be next to us, the person most in need of our help. Whether he is related to us or not, whether we "like" him or not, doesn't make any difference.

ST. EDITH STEIN (20TH C.)

51

Jesus is honey in the mouth, music in the ear, and a shout of joy in the heart.

ST. BERNARD OF CLAIRVAUX (12th C.)

52

Do not seek to be regarded as somebody, don't compare yourself to others in anything.

ST. BARSANUPHIUS (6TH C.)

53

What was the first rule of our dear Savior's life? You know it was to do his Father's will. Well, then, the first end I propose in our daily work is to do the will of God. Secondly, do it in the manner he willed, and finally, do it because it is his will.

ST. ELIZABETH BAYLEY SETON (19TH C.)

54

A glad spirit attains to perfection more quickly than any other.

ST. PHILIP NERI (16TH C.)

55

Who except God can give you peace? Has the world ever been able to satisfy the heart?

ST. GERARD MAJELLA (18TH C.)

56

When I do reflect within myself, I do sometimes perceive most clearly
that those persons who do best know God (who is infinite and
unspeakable) are those who do the least presume to speak of him, con-
sidering that all which they do say of him, or possibly can say, is as
nothing compared with what he truly is.

BL. ANGELA OF FOLIGNO (13TH C.)

57

No one can live without delight and that is why a man deprived of
spiritual joy goes over to carnal pleasures.

ST. THOMAS AQUINAS (13TH C.)

58

I have been made for heaven and heaven for me.

ST. JOSEPH CAFASSO (19TH C.)

59

To be loved by God, to be united to God, to live in the presence of God, to live for God! Oh! how wonderful life is—and death!

ST. JOHN VIANNEY (19TH C.)

60

If I saw the gates of hell open and I stood on the brink of the abyss, I should not despair, I should not lose hope of mercy, because I should trust in thee, my God.

St. Gemma Galgani (19th c.)

61

Man's body has acquired something great through its communion and union with the Word. From being mortal it has been made immortal; though it was a living body it has become a spiritual one; though it was made from the earth it has passed through the gates of heaven.

St. Athanasius (4th c.)

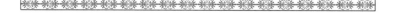

62

A young village girl told me, When I am about to talk to anyone, I picture to myself Jesus Christ and how gracious and friendly he was to everyone.

ST. JOHN VIANNEY (19TH C.)

63

There is no more excellent way to obtain graces from God than to seek them through Mary, because her Divine Son cannot refuse her anything.

ST. PHILIP NERI (16TH C.)

64

The Christian prays in every situation, in his walks for recreation, in his dealings with others, in silence, in reading, in all rational pursuits.

ST. CLEMENT OF ALEXANDRIA (2ND C.)

65

Our labor here is brief, but the reward is eternal. Do not be disturbed by the clamor of the world, which passes like a shadow. Do not let the false delights of a deceptive world deceive you.

ST. CLARE OF ASSISI (13TH C.)

66

The past must be abandoned to God's mercy, the present to our fidelity, the future to divine providence.

ST. FRANCIS DE SALES (17TH C.)

67

For me, prayer means launching out of the heart toward God; it means lifting up one's eyes, quite simply, to heaven, a cry of grateful love from the crest of joy or the trough of despair; it's a vast, supernatural force which opens out my heart, and binds me close to Jesus.

ST. THÉRÈSE OF LISIEUX (19TH C.)

68

God is more anxious to bestow his blessings on us than we are to receive them.

ST. AUGUSTINE OF HIPPO (5TH C.)

69

This was the method that Christ used with the apostles. He put up with their ignorance and roughness and even their infidelity. He treated sinners with kindness and affection so that he caused some to be shocked, others to be scandalized, and still others to hope for God's mercy. And so he commanded us to be gentle and humble of heart.

ST. JOHN BOSCO (19TH C.)

70

There is no sin nor wrong that gives a man such a foretaste of hell in this life as anger and impatience.

ST. CATHERINE OF SIENA (14TH C.)

71

Comfort in tribulation can be secured only on the sure ground of faith holding as true the words of Scripture and the teaching of the Catholic church.

ST. THOMAS MORE (16TH C.)

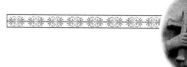

72

Faith is the proof of what cannot be seen. What is seen gives knowledge, not faith.

ST. GREGORY THE GREAT (6TH C.)

73

Granting that we are always in the presence of God, yet it seems to me that those who pray are in his presence in a very different sense; for they, as it were, see that he is looking upon them, while others may be for days together without even once recollecting that God sees them.

ST. TERESA OF AVILA (16TH C.)

74

If I want only pure water, what does it matter to me whether it be brought in a vase of gold or of glass? What is it to me whether the will of God be presented to me in tribulation or consolation, since I desire and seek only the Divine Will?

ST. FRANCIS DE SALES (17TH C.)

75

I will not mistrust him ... though I shall feel myself weakening and on the verge of being overcome with fear. I shall remember how St. Peter at a blast of wind began to sink because of his lack of faith, and I shall do as he did: call upon Christ and pray to him for help. And then I trust he shall place his holy hand on me and in the stormy seas hold me up from drowning.

ST. THOMAS MORE (16TH C.)

76

Let us study, then, how to bear worldly tribulations with patience, yes, even with cheerfulness, because herein lies the sign that the Beloved delights in us and has chosen us and will give us the pledge of his inheritance.

BL. ANGELA OF FOLIGNO (13TH C.)

77

You must accept your cross; if you carry it courageously it will carry you to heaven.

ST. JOHN VIANNEY (19TH C.)

78

When you see our heads fixed up over the bridge, think that they are there to preach to you the very same faith for which we are about to die.

St. Alban Roe (17th c.)

79

Yesterday, on approaching the Most Blessed Sacrament, I felt myself burning and I had to withdraw. I am astounded that so many who receive Jesus are not reduced to ashes.

St. Gemma Galgani (19th c.)

80

Waves lash at the Church but do not shatter it. Although the elements of this world constantly batter and crash against her, she offers the safest harbor of salvation for all in distress.

ST. AMBROSE (4TH C.)

81

When did it ever happen that a person had confidence in God and was lost?

ST. ALPHONSUS LIGUORI (18TH C.)

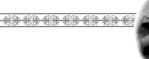

82

There's no respect for poor, wretched women anywhere. And yet you'll find the love of God much commoner among women than among men, and the women at the Crucifixion showed much more courage than the apostles, exposing themselves to insult and wiping our Lord's face.

ST. THÉRÈSE OF LISIEUX (19TH C.)

83

Your way of acting should be different from the world's way; the love of Christ must come before all else. You are not to act in anger or nurse a grudge. Rid your heart of all deceit. Never give a hollow greeting of peace or turn away when someone needs your love.

ST. BENEDICT OF NURSIA (6TH C.)

84

Our Lord has created persons for all states in life, and in all of them we see people who have achieved sanctity by fulfilling their obligations well.

St. Anthony Mary Claret (19th c.)

85

We have a long way to go to heaven, and as many good deeds as we do, as many prayers as we make, and as many good thoughts as we think in truth and hope and charity, so many paces do we go heaven-ward.

Bl. Richard Rolle (14th c.)

86

Like a farmer tending a sound tree, untouched by ax or fire because of its fruit, I want to serve you good people, not only in the body, but also to give my life for your well-being.

ST. EUSEBIUS OF VERCELLI (4TH C.)

87

I took the opportunity to give him a good brotherly reproof, putting him in mind of the rule of St. Francis about simplicity in teaching. Then, to sweeten the medicine, I sent him some trout.

ST. ROBERT BELLARMINE (17TH C.)

88

The better friends you are, the straighter you can talk, but while you are only on nodding terms, be slow to scold.

ST. FRANCIS XAVIER (16TH C.)

89

Reject absolutely all divination, fortune-telling, sacrifices to the dead, prophesies in groves or by fountains, amulets, incantation, sorcery (that is wicked enchantments), and all those sacrilegious practices which used to go on in your country.

ST. GREGORY III (8TH C.)

90

As regards certain customs of these savages, do not try to belittle them, but rather, after the example of the Church in ancient times amidst pagan peoples, try to sanctify such customs, provided they are not harmful to soul or body.

BL. MICHAEL RUA (19TH C.)

91

If indeed the race of the English—as is noised abroad and is cast up to us in France and Italy—spurn lawful wedlock, a people unworthy and degenerate will be born and the nation will cease to be strong. We suffer for the disgraceful conduct of our people.

ST. BONIFACE (8TH C.)

92

Nothing richer can be offered to God than a good will; for the good will is the originator of all good and is the mother of all virtues; whosoever begins to have that good will has secured all the help he needs for living well.

ST. ALBERT THE GREAT (13TH C.)

93

Let none of you take a merely natural attitude toward his neighbor, but love one another continually in Jesus Christ.

ST. IGNATIUS OF ANTIOCH (2ND C.)

94

Poverty was not found in heaven. It abounded on earth, but man did not know its value. The Son of God, therefore, treasured it and came down from heaven to choose it for himself, to make it precious to us.

ST. BERNARD OF CLAIRVAUX (12TH C.)

95

Blessed is the servant who esteems himself no better when he is praised and exalted by people than when he is considered worthless, simple, and despicable; for what a man is before God, that he is and nothing more.

ST. FRANCIS OF ASSISI (13TH C.)

96

We were born to love, we live to love, and we will die to love still more.

ST. JOSEPH CAFASSO (19TH C.)

97

The sooner you forgive him, the sooner he will recover from his illness. You are the person to restore him to health of soul and body.

ST. CATHERINE DEI RICCI (16TH C.)

98

Every evil is based on some good. Indeed, evil cannot exist by itself, since it has no essence, as we have shown. Therefore, evil must be in some subject. Now, every subject, because it is some sort of substance, is a good of some kind. So, every evil is in a good thing.

ST. THOMAS AQUINAS (13TH C.)

99

Just as water extinguishes a fire, so love wipes away sin.

ST. JOHN OF GOD (16TH C.)

100

Works of mercy done either to ourselves or to our neighbor and
referred to God are true sacrifices. Works of mercy are performed for
no other reason than to free us from wretchedness and by this means
to make us happy.

ST. AUGUSTINE OF HIPPO (5TH C.)

101

Truly I tell you that no one should consider himself a perfect friend of
God until he has passed through many temptations and tribulations.

ST. FRANCIS OF ASSISI (13TH C.)

102

God commands you to pray, but he fobids you to *worry*.

ST. JOHN VIANNEY (19TH C.)

103

Men can heal the lustful. Angels can heal the malicious. Only God can heal the proud.

ST. JOHN CLIMACUS (7TH C.)

104

On people who claim to have messages direct from God: "God told me, God replied to me," they assert and yet most of the time they are talking to themselves.

ST. JOHN OF THE CROSS (16TH C.)

105

Riches are the instrument of all vices, because they render us capable of putting even our worst desires into execution.

ST. AMBROSE (4TH C.)

106

I am but a poor little thing who would return to nothingness if your divine glance did not give me life from one moment to the next.

ST. THÉRÈSE OF LISIEUX (19TH C.)

107

Take even bread with moderation, lest an overloaded stomach make you weary of prayer.

ST. BERNARD OF CLAIRVAUX (12TH C.)

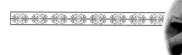

108

The soul should treat the body as its child, correcting without hurting it.

ST. FRANCIS DE SALES (17TH C.)

109

Just as at sea those who are carried away from the direction of the harbor bring themselves back on course by a clear sign, on seeing a tall beacon light or some mountain peak coming into view, so Scripture may guide those adrift on the sea of life back into the harbor of the divine will.

ST. GREGORY OF NYSSA (4TH C.)

110

God made me understand that there are souls that his mercy does not tire of waiting for, to whom he gives his light by degrees. Also, I was careful not to move his time ahead, and I waited patiently until it pleases Jesus to make it come.

ST. THÉRÈSE OF LISIEUX (19TH C.)

111

I desire to love You, my Lord, my Light, / my strength, my deliverer, my God and my All. / What have I in heaven, O God, what do I want besides you on earth? / My spirit and my body languish with yearning for your majesty. / You are the God of my heart; You are my portion, my inheritance for eternity. Amen.

ST. PASCHAL BAYLON (16TH C.)

112

Never take a man for your example in the tasks you have to perform, however holy he may be. Imitate Christ, who is supremely perfect and supremely holy, and you will never err.

ST. JOHN OF THE CROSS (16TH C.)

113

Greatly should we rejoice that God dwells in our soul—and rejoice yet more because our soul dwells in God. Our soul is created to be God's home, and the soul is at home in the uncreated God.

BL. JULIAN OF NORWICH (15TH C.)

114

Every time I do not behave like a donkey, it is the worse for me. How does a donkey behave? If it is slandered, it keeps silent; if it is not fed, it keeps silent; if it is forgotten, it keeps silent; it never complains, however much it is beaten or ill-used, because it has a donkey's patience. That is how the servant of God must behave. I stand before you, Lord, like a donkey.

ST. PETER CLAVER (17TH C.)

115

Just as God's creature, the sun, is one and the same the world over, so also does the Church's preaching shine everywhere to enlighten all men who want to come to a knowledge of truth.

ST. IRENAEUS (2ND C.)

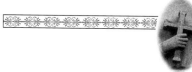

116

Be kind to all and severe to yourself.

ST. TERESA OF AVILA (16TH C.)

117

There are certain souls who are always looking for consolation in prayer; this is a delusion of the devil, who simply wishes to bring about their destruction.

ST. ALPHONSUS LIGUORI (18TH C.)

118

Leave sadness to those in the world. We who work for God should be lighthearted.

ST. LEONARD OF PORT MAURICE (17TH C.)

119

Do not grieve or complain that you were born in a time when you can no longer see God in the flesh. He did not in fact take this privilege from you. As he says, "Whatever you have done to the least of my brothers, you did to me."

ST. AUGUSTINE OF HIPPO (5TH C.)

120

Come, let us offer Christ the great, universal sacrifice of our love, and pour out before him our richest hymns and prayers.

ST. EPHREM OF SYRIA (4TH C.)

121

True humility makes no pretense of being humble, and scarcely ever utters words of humility.

ST. FRANCIS DE SALES (17TH C.)

122

To reach something good it is very useful to have gone astray, and thus acquire experience.

ST. TERESA OF AVILA (16TH C.)

123

The noblest sacrament ... is that wherein his Body is really present. The Eucharist crowns all the other sacraments.

ST. THOMAS AQUINAS (13TH C.)

124

Let justice be done though the world perish.

ST. AUGUSTINE OF HIPPO (5TH C.)

125

Faithfulness in little things is a big thing.

ST. JOHN CHRYSOSTOM (5TH C.)

126

I have lived a long time, and the righteous Judge has taken good care of me during my whole life.

ST. BEDE THE VENERABLE (8TH C.)

127

Our home is heaven. On earth we are like travelers staying at a hotel. When one is away, one is always thinking of going home.

ST. JOHN VIANNEY (19TH C.)

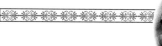

128

God, the Lord and Maker of all things, who created the world and set it in order, not only loved us but was patient with us. So He has always been, and is, and will ever be: kind, good, free from anger, truthful—indeed, he and he alone is good.

ST. JUSTIN MARTYR (2ND C.)

129

Then I saw truly that it gives more praise to God and more delight if we pray steadfast in love, trusting his goodness, clinging to him by grace, than if we ask for everything our thoughts can name.

BL. JULIAN OF NORWICH (15TH C.)

130

God does not listen to the prayers of the lazy.

ST. SIXTUS I (2ND C.)

131

In all those things which do not come under the obligation of faith, the saints were at liberty to hold divergent views, just as we ourselves are.

ST. THOMAS AQUINAS (13TH C.)

132

Let us love God, but with the strength of our arms, in the sweat of our brow.

ST. VINCENT DE PAUL (17TH C.)

133

He did submit himself unto the elements, unto cold and heat, hunger and thirst, and other insensible creatures, concealing his power and despoiling himself thereof in the likeness of man, in order that he might teach us weak and wretched mortals with what patience we ought to bear tribulation.

BL. ANGELA OF FOLIGNO (13TH C.)

134

Out of love the Lord took us to himself; because he loved us and it was God's will, our Lord Jesus Christ gave his life's blood for us—he gave his body for our body, his soul for our soul.

St. Clement of Rome (2nd c.)

135

Hope everything from the mercy of God. It is as boundless as his power.

St. Frances of Rome (14th c.)

136

You are poor? But there are others poorer than you. You have enough to keep you alive for ten days—but this man has enough for only one.... Don't be afraid to give away the little that you have. Don't put your own interests before the common good. Give your last loaf to the beggar at your door, and trust in God's goodness.

ST. BASIL THE GREAT (4TH C.)

137

Men are so like frogs. They go open-mouthed for the lure of things which do not concern them, and that wily angler the devil knows how to capture multitudes of them.

ST. ROBERT BELLARMINE (17TH C.)

138

Nothing half-hearted for me—I will follow Christ with all my heart and soul.

ST. THÉRÈSE OF LISIEUX (19TH C.)

139

Let women make up their own minds.

ST. GREGORY THE GREAT (6TH C.)

140

God does not insist or desire that we should mourn in agony of heart; rather, it is his wish that out of love for him we should rejoice with laughter in our soul.

ST. JOHN CLIMACUS (7TH C.)

141

I do not bless war: I bless peace.

ST. PIUS X (20TH C.)

142

You should never judge sinners, you should never despise them, for you know not the judgments of God.

BL. ANGELA OF FOLIGNO (13TH C.)

143

God deliver us from sullen saints!

ST. TERESA OF AVILA (16TH C.)

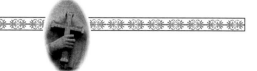

144

I pray you, noble Jesus, that as you have graciously granted me joyfully to drink the words of your knowledge, so you will also of your goodness grant me to come at length to yourself, the fount of all wisdom, and to dwell in your presence forever.

ST. BEDE THE VENERABLE (8TH C.)

145

A Christian should always remember that the value of his good works is not based on their number and excellence, but on the love of God which prompts him to do these things.

ST. JOHN OF THE CROSS (16TH C.)

146

Christians are made, not born.

ST. JEROME (4TH C.)

147

You will effect more by kind words and by a courteous manner, than by anger or sharp rebuke, which should never be used but in necessity.

ST. ANGELA MERICI (16TH C.)

148

Christ shines into the bottom of the humble heart; for Christ is always moved by helplessness whenever a man complains of it and lays it before him with humility.

BL. JAN VAN RUYSBROECK (14TH C.)

149

Those who torment themselves with eagerness and anxiety do little, and that badly.

ST. FRANCIS DE SALES (17TH C.)

150

God is within all things, but not included; outside all things, but not excluded; above all things, but not beyond their reach.

ST. GREGORY THE GREAT (6TH C.)

151

It is right to submit to higher authority whenever a command of God would not be violated.

ST. BASIL THE GREAT (4TH C.)

152

As the body is clad in clothes, and the flesh in the skin, and the bones in the flesh, and the heart in the whole, so are we clothed, body and soul, in the goodness of God and enfolded in it.

BL. JULIAN OF NORWICH (15TH C.)

153

Understanding is the reward of faith. Therefore seek not to understand that you may believe, but believe that you may understand.

ST. AUGUSTINE OF HIPPO (5TH C.)

154

Make yourself a seller when you are buying, and a buyer when you are selling, and then you will sell and buy justly.

ST. FRANCIS DE SALES (17TH C.)

155

To be a Christian is a great thing, not merely to seem one. And somehow or other those please the world most who please Christ the least.

ST. JEROME (4TH C.)

156

Holy Communion is the shortest and safest way to heaven.

ST. PIUS X (20TH C.)

157

The greater and more persistent your confidence in God, the more abundantly you will receive all that you ask.

ST. ALBERT THE GREAT (13TH C.)

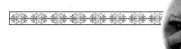

158

Consider every day that you are then for the first time—as it were—beginning; and always act with the same fervor as on the first day you began.

St. Anthony of Padua (13th c.)

159

Blessed be God for our sister, the death of the body.

St. Francis of Assisi (13th c.)

160

Do you hate to be deceived? Then never deceive another.

ST. JOHN CHRYSOSTOM (5TH C.)

161

Down with all melancholy. That should never find a place except in the heart which has lost faith. I am joyful. Sorrow is not gloom. Gloom should be banished from the Christian soul.

PIER-GIORGIO FRASSATI (20TH C.)

162

The Virgin Mary has become the advocate for the Virgin Eve. Death was brought upon the world by a virgin; life has triumphed by the Virgin Mary's obedience, which has finally balanced the debt of disobedience.

St. Irenaeus (2nd c.)

163

Happy is the one who has been able to cut out that root of vice, avarice.... What do superfluous riches profit in this world when they do not assist our birth or impede our dying? We are born into this world naked; we leave it without a cent; we are buried without our inheritance.

St. Ambrose (4th c.)

164

Truly you, O Mary, are blessed among all women, because while remaining a woman, a creature of our race, you have become the Mother of God. For if the Holy One born of your womb is truly God incarnate, you must truly be called the Mother of God, since you have, in absolute truth, brought forth God.

ST. SOPHRONIUS (7TH C.)

165

O God, let me know you and love you so that I may find my joy in you; and if I cannot do so fully in this life, let me at least make some progress daily, until at last that knowledge, love, and joy come to me in all their plenitude in heaven.

ST. ANSELM (12TH C.)

166

Actions speak louder than words; let your words teach and your actions speak.

ST. ANTHONY OF PADUA (13TH C.)

167

Virgin most patient, grant us patience amid the trials and sorrows so plentiful in this world, so that after the storm of adversities, afflictions, and anguish which everywhere assail us, we may with joy reach the land of the living, the haven of eternal beatitude, there to enjoy the everlasting rest prepared for the elect.

ST. JOAN OF VALOIS (16TH C.)

168

Christ hungers now, my brethren; it is he who deigns to hunger and
thirst in the persons of the poor. And what he will return in heaven
tomorrow is what he receives here on earth today.

ST. CAESARIUS OF ARLES (6TH C.)

169

I resolved always to prefer labors to comforts, contempt to honors.
And, in particular, if on one side a kingdom were offered and on the
other the washing of dishes, I would refuse the kingdom and accept
the dish-washing so as to be truly like Christ, who humbled himself.

ST. JOHN BERCHMANS (17TH C.)

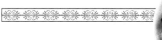

170

There is a spiritual life that we share with the angels of heaven and with the divine spirits, for like them we have been formed in the image and likeness of God.

ST. LAWRENCE OF BRINDISI (16TH C.)

171

All the ways of this world are as fickle and unstable as a sudden storm at sea.

ST. BEDE THE VENERABLE (8TH C.)

172

The eyes of this world see no further than this life, as mine see no further than this wall when the church door is shut. The eyes of the Christian see deep into eternity.

ST. JOHN VIANNEY (19TH C.)

173

The earth was made for all, rich and poor, in common. Why do you rich claim it as your exclusive right?

ST. AMBROSE (4TH C.)

174

You can love this life all you want, as long as you know what to choose.

ST. AUGUSTINE OF HIPPO (5TH C.)

175

Do well what you can, and the rest leave to God, who will do it sooner or later, according to the disposition of his divine providence.

ST. FRANCIS DE SALES (17TH C.)

176

If I look at myself I am nothing. But if I look at us all I am hopeful; for I see the unity of love among all my fellow-Christians. In this unity lies our salvation.

BL. JULIAN OF NORWICH (15TH C.)

177

O Lord, only grant me love for you and I shall be rich enough. I desire only that you leave me to my nothingness and that you alone, if I may say so, be all in all and loved and honored by everyone. I wish to take pleasure in nothing but only in you and in your love. Amen.

BL. CRESCENTIA HÖSS (17TH C.)

178

Nothing is so strong as gentleness, nothing so gentle as real strength.

ST. FRANCIS DE SALES (17TH C.)

179

And when night comes, and you look back over the day and see how fragmentary everything has been, and how much you planned that has gone undone, and all the reasons you have to be embarrassed and ashamed: just take everything exactly as it is, put it in God's hands and leave it with him. Then you will be able to rest in him—really rest— and start the next day as a new life.

ST. EDITH STEIN (20TH C.)

180

Cast yourself into the arms of God and be very sure that if he wants
anything of you, he will fit you for the work and give you strength.

ST. PHILIP NERI (16TH C.)

181

It shows weakness of mind to hold too much to the beaten track
through fear of innovations. Times change and to keep up with them,
we must modify our methods.

ST. MADELEINE SOPHIE BARAT (19TH C.)

182

Our Lord and Savior lifted up his voice and said with incomparable majesty: "Let all men know that grace comes after tribulation. Let them know that without the burden of afflictions it is impossible to reach the height of grace. Let them know that the gifts of grace increase as the struggles increase."

ST. ROSE OF LIMA (16TH C.)

183

Countless numbers are deceived in multiplying prayers. I would rather say five words devoutly and with my heart than five thousand which my soul does not relish with affection and understanding.

ST. EDMUND THE MARTYR (9TH C.)

184

There is no such thing as bad weather. All weather is good because it is God's.

ST. TERESA OF AVILA (16TH C.)

185

My little children, your hearts are small, but prayer stretches them and makes them capable of loving God. Through prayer we receive a fore-taste of heaven and something of paradise comes down upon us.

ST. JOHN VIANNEY (19TH C.)

186

Assist me, my Jesus, for I desire to become good whatsoever it may cost; take away, destroy, utterly root out all that you find in me contrary to your holy will. At the same time, I pray you, Lord Jesus, to enlighten me that I may be able to walk in your holy light. Amen.

ST. GEMMA GALGANI (19TH C.)

187

Fortify me with the grace of your Holy Spirit and give your peace to my soul that I may be free from all needless anxiety, solicitude, and worry. Help me to desire always that which is pleasing and acceptable to you so that your will may be my will.

ST. FRANCES XAVIER CABRINI (20TH C.)

188

Prayer should ... be short and pure, unless perhaps it is prolonged under the inspiration of divine grace.

ST. BENEDICT OF NURSIA (6TH C.)

189

Be not anxious about what you have but about what you are.

ST. GREGORY THE GREAT (6TH C.)

190

What brings joy to the heart is not so much the friend's gift as the friend's love.

ST. AILRED OF RIEVAULX (12TH C.)

191

Provided that God be glorified, we must not care by whom.

ST. FRANCIS DE SALES (17TH C.)

192

Grace does not destroy nature, it perfects it.

ST. THOMAS AQUINAS (13TH C.)

193

Ingratitude is the soul's enemy; it empties it of merit, scatters its virtues, and deprives it of graces.

ST. BERNARD OF CLAIRVAUX (12TH C.)

194

Happiness is the practice of the virtues.

ST. CLEMENT OF ALEXANDRIA (2ND C.)

195

Be careful to preserve your health. It is a trick of the devil, which he employs to deceive good souls, to incite them to do more than they are able, in order that they may no longer be able to do anything.

ST. VINCENT DE PAUL (17TH C.)

196

Every truth without exception and whoever may utter it is from the Holy Spirit. The old pagan virtues were from God. Revelation has been made to many pagans.

ST. THOMAS AQUINAS (13TH C.)

197

God is full of compassion and never fails those who are afflicted and despised if they trust in him alone.

ST. TERESA OF AVILA (16TH C.)

198

He who trusts in himself is lost. He who trusts in God can do all things.

ST. ALPHONSUS LIGUORI (18TH C.)

199

A few acts of confidence and love are worth more than a thousand "who knows? who knows?" Heaven is filled with converted sinners of all kinds and there is room for more.

ST. JOSEPH CAFASSO (19TH C.)

200

If you wish to make any progress in the service of God we must begin every day of our life with new ardor.

ST. CHARLES BORROMEO (16TH C.)

201

O man, believe in God with all your might, for hope rests on faith, love on hope, and victory on love; the reward will follow victory, the crown of life the reward, but the crown is the essence of things eternal.

ST. NICHOLAS OF FLÜE (15TH C.)

202

In whatever way it seems best to you to please the Lord God, and to follow his footprints and his poverty, do this with the blessing of God.

ST. FRANCIS OF ASSISI (13TH C.)

203

Let us learn to cast our hearts into God.

ST. BERNARD OF CLAIRVAUX (12TH C.)

204

All the way to heaven is heaven, because Jesus said, "I am the way."

ST. CATHERINE OF SIENA (14TH C.)

205

All of us can attain to Christian virtue and holiness, no matter in what condition of life we live and no matter what our lifework may be.

ST. FRANCIS DE SALES (17TH C.)

206

I saw in truth that God does all things, however small they may be. And I saw that nothing happens by chance, but by the farsighted wisdom of God. If it seems like chance to us, it is because we are blind and blinkered.

BL. JULIAN OF NORWICH (15TH C.)

207

No one heals himself by wounding another.

ST. AMBROSE (4TH C.)

208

God is all to you: if you are hungry, he is bread; if thirsty, he is water; if darkness, he is light; if naked, he is a robe of immortality.

ST. AUGUSTINE OF HIPPO (5TH C.)

209

With God, we should feel like a child in its mother's arms; if he carries us on the left arm or the right, it is all the same to us, we let him do what he wants.

ST. FRANCIS DE SALES (17TH C.)

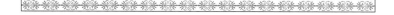

210

Language comes alive when it speaks by deeds. Enough of talking; let actions speak. We are bloated with words and empty works.

ST. ANTHONY OF PADUA (13TH C.)

211

You should bear patiently the bad temper of other people, the slights, the rudeness that may be offered you.

ST. JOHN BOSCO (19TH C.)

212

If you have seen your brother, you have seen God.

ST. CLEMENT OF ALEXANDRIA (2ND C.)

213

The gate of heaven is very low; only the humble can enter it.

ST. ELIZABETH ANN SETON (19TH C.)

214

Christ has no body now on earth, but yours, no hands but yours, no feet but yours; yours are the eyes through which is to look out Christ's compassion to the world, yours are the feet with which he is to go about doing good, and yours are the hands with which he is to bless us now.

St. Teresa of Avila (16th c.)

215

God loves all existing things.

St. Thomas Aquinas (13th c.)

216

The human body has been greatly enhanced through the fellowship
and union of the Word with it.

ST. ATHANASIUS (4TH C.)

217

The Father most tender, Father of All, my immense God—I his atom.

ST. ELIZABETH SETON (18TH C.)

218

Prudence must precede every action that we undertake; for, if prudence be wanting, there is nothing, however good it may seem, which is not turned into evil.

ST. BASIL THE GREAT (4TH C.)

219

We are too little to be able always to rise above difficulties. Well, then, let us pass beneath them quite simply.

ST. THÉRÈSE OF LISIEUX (19TH C.)

220

When I am before the Blessed Sacrament I feel such a lively faith that I can't describe it. Christ in the Eucharist is almost tangible to me.... When it's time for me to leave, I have to tear myself away from his sacred presence.

ST. ANTHONY MARY CLARET (19TH C.)

221

For where the Church is, there is the Spirit of God; and where the Spirit of God is, there is the Church and every form of grace, for the Spirit is truth.

ST. IRENAEUS (2ND C.)

222

Be a John the Baptist to the incestuous, a Phineas to those who apostatize and go whoring, a Peter to liars, a Paul to blasphemers, a Christ to traitors.

ST. PETER MARTYR (13TH C.)

223

Until Mary Immaculate, the Woman *par excellence*, foretold by the prophets ... has appeared on earth, what was woman? But Mary appeared ... and a new era arose for woman. She was no longer a slave but equal to man.... All this we owe to Mary.

ST. FRANCES XAVIER CABRINI (20TH C.)

224

It is untrue that the saints were not like us. They too experienced temptations, they fell and rose again; they experienced sorrow that weakened and paralyzed them with a sense of discouragement.

ST. MAXIMILIAN KOLBE (20TH C.)

225

Good works are the most perfect when they are wrought in the most pure and sincere love of God, and with the least regard to our own present and future interests, or to joy and sweetness, consolation or praise.

ST. JOHN OF THE CROSS (16TH C.)

226

I imagine the angels themselves, if they came down as schoolmasters, would find it hard to control their anger. Only with the help of the Blessed Virgin do I keep from murdering some of them [i.e. students].

ST. BENILDUS (19TH C.)

227

The saints had no bitterness, no hatred. They forgave everything.

ST. JOHN VIANNEY (19TH C.)

228

Where the sign of the cross occurs, magic loses its power, and sorcery has no effect.

ST. ANTHONY OF EGYPT (3RD C.)

229

Sanctify yourself and you will sanctify society.

ST. FRANCIS OF ASSISI (13TH C.)

230

The Christian should offer his brethren simple and unpretentious hospitality.

ST. BASIL THE GREAT (4TH C.)

231

Poor creature though I be, I am the hand and foot of Christ. I move my hand and my hand is wholly Christ's hand, for deity is become inseparably one with me. I move my foot, and it is aglow with God.

ST. SYMEON THE NEW THEOLOGIAN (10TH C.)

232

Humility is the mother of salvation.

ST. BERNARD OF CLAIRVAUX (12TH C.)

233

The Word of God, Jesus Christ, on account of his great love for mankind, became what we are in order to make us what He is himself.

ST. IRENAEUS (2ND C.)

234

When it seems that God shows us the faults of others, keep on the safer side. It may be that your judgment is false.

ST. CATHERINE OF SIENA (14TH C.)

235

The rule of justice is plain, namely, that a good man ought not to swerve from the truth, not to inflict any unjust loss on anyone, nor to act in any way deceitfully or fraudulently.

ST. AMBROSE (4TH C.)

236

A scrap of knowledge about sublime things is worth more than any amount about trivialities.

ST. THOMAS AQUINAS (13TH C.)

237

It is God's will that we should rejoice with him in our salvation, and that we should be cheered and strengthened by it. He wants our soul to delight in its salvation, through his grace. For we are the apple of his eye.

BL. JULIAN OF NORWICH (15TH C.)

238

In the childhood of the spiritual life, when we first entrust ourselves to God's providence, God's guiding hand feels very strong and firm. We know as clear as day what we should or shouldn't do. But things don't stay like this forever.

ST. EDITH STEIN (20TH C.)

239

What deep mysteries ... are contained in the Lord's Prayer! How many and great they are! They are expressed in a few words but they are rich in spiritual power so that nothing is left out; every petition and prayer we have to make is included. It is a compendium of heavenly doctrine.

ST. CYPRIAN (3RD C.)

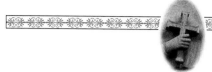

240

The rich man is not one who is in possession of much, but one who gives much.

ST. JOHN CHRYSOSTOM (5TH C.)

241

Faith is to believe what we do not see, and the reward of this faith is to see what we believe.

ST. AUGUSTINE OF HIPPO (5TH C.)

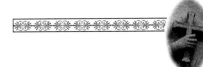

242

Holiness is not one exercise or another, it consists in a disposition of the heart, which renders us humble and little in the hands of God, conscious of our weakness but confident, even daringly confident, in his fatherly goodness.

ST. THÉRÈSE OF LISIEUX (19TH C.)

243

Do now, do now, what you will wish to have done when your moment comes to die.

ST. ANGELA MERICI (16TH C.)

244

We can do nothing unless divine aid supports us. This divine aid is at hand for all who seek it with truly humble and devout heart.

ST. BONAVENTURE (13TH C.)

245

If you want God to hear your prayers, hear the voice of the poor. If you wish God to anticipate your wants, provide those of the needy without waiting for them to ask you. Especially anticipate the needs of those who are ashamed to beg. To make them ask for alms is to make them buy it.

ST. THOMAS OF VILLANOVA (15TH C.)

246

Anyone who belongs to Christ is destined to pass through all the stages of his life—up to and including his adulthood, and eventually, even to the way of the Cross that leads to Gethsemane and Golgotha.

ST. EDITH STEIN (20TH C.)

247

All the merit of virtue lies in the will. Sometimes a man who wishes to believe has more merit than another who does believe.

ST. ALPHONSUS LIGUORI (18TH C.)

248

If you truly want to help the soul of your neighbor, you should approach God first with all your heart. Ask him simply to fill you with charity, the greatest of all the virtues; with it you can accomplish what you desire.

ST. VINCENT FERRER (14TH C.)

249

If you would rise, shun luxury, for luxury lowers and degrades.

ST. JOHN CHRYSOSTOM (5TH C.)

250

The soul cannot live without love. All depends on providing it with a worthy object.

ST. FRANCIS DE SALES (17TH C.)

251

You may be certain of this: if you practice love within your own family, God will help you outside it.

ST. ALPHONSUS LIGUORI (18TH C.)

252

Remember that nothing is small in the eyes of God. Do all that you do with love.

ST. THÉRÈSE OF LISIEUX (19TH C.)

253

When you receive a letter from a friend, you should not delay to embrace it as a friend. For it is a fine consolation among the absent that if a loved one is not present, a letter may be embraced instead.

ST. ISIDORE OF SEVILLE (7TH C.)

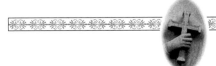

254

Do not think that your crosses are tremendous, that they are tests of your fidelity to God and tokens of God's extraordinary love for you. This thought has its source in spiritual pride.... You ought to acknowledge that you are so proud and sensitive that you magnify straws into rafters, scratches into deep wounds, rats into elephants.

ST. LOUIS-MARIE GRIGNION DE MONTFORT (17TH C.)

255

There is nothing small in the service of God.

ST. FRANCIS DE SALES (17TH C.)

256

It is a great thing, this reading of the Scriptures! For it is not possible ever to exhaust the mind of the Scriptures. It is a well that has no bottom.

ST. JOHN CHRYSOSTOM (5TH C.)

257

Cursed be that loyalty which reaches so far as to go against the law of God.

ST. TERESA OF AVILA (16TH C.)

258

Because of our good Lord's tender love to all those who shall be saved, he quickly comforts them, saying, "The cause of all this pain is sin. But all shall be well, and all shall be well, and all manner of thing shall be well." These words were said so kindly and without a hint of blame.... So how unjust it would be for me to blame God for allowing my sin when he does not blame me for falling into it.

Bl. Julian of Norwich (15th c.)

259

Each of us is perpetually on the razor's edge: on one side, absolute nothingness; on the other, the fullness of divine life.

St. Edith Stein (20th c.)

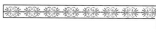

260

My daughter, I see more Pharisees among the Christians than there were around Pilate.

ST. MARGARET OF CORTONA (13TH C.)

261

Let us look at our own shortcomings and leave other people's alone; for those who live carefully ordered lives are apt to be shocked at everything, and we might well learn very important lessons from the persons who shock us.

ST. TERESA OF AVILA (16TH C.)

262

Our relentless enemy, the teacher of fornication, whispers that God is lenient and particularly merciful to this passion, since it is so very natural. Yet if we watch the wiles of the demons we will observe that after we have actually sinned they will affirm that God is a just and inexorable judge. They say one thing to lead us into sin, another thing to overwhelm us in despair.

St. John Climacus (7th c.)

263

The love of worldly possessions is a sort of birdlime, which entangles the soul and prevents it flying to God.

St. Augustine of Hippo (5th c.)

264

Irrational feeding darkens the soul and makes it unfit for spiritual experiences.

St. Thomas Aquinas (13th c.)

265

Do you not know that fasting can master concupiscence, lift up the soul, confirm it in the paths of virtue, and prepare a fine reward for the Christian?

St. Hedwig of Silesia (13th c.)

266

What moved and stimulated me most was reading the Holy Bible, to which I have always been very strongly attracted. There were passages that impressed me so deeply that I seemed to hear a voice telling me the message I was reading.

ST. ANTHONY MARY CLARET (19TH C.)

267

The state of marriage is one that requires more virtue and constancy than any other; it is a perpetual exercise in mortification.

ST. FRANCIS DE SALES (17TH C.)

268

Let us not imagine that we obscure the glory of the Son by the praise we lavish on the Mother; for the more she is honored, the greater is the glory of her Son.

ST. BERNARD OF CLAIRVAUX (12TH C.)

269

Mercy, also, is a good thing, for it makes men perfect, in that it imitates the perfect Father. Nothing graces the Christian soul so much as mercy.

ST. AMBROSE (4TH C.)

270

The one thing a person needs to keep doing is to try to live out his chosen vocation with an ever-increasing honesty and purity.

ST. EDITH STEIN (20TH C.)

271

The Lord came not to make a display, but to teach and heal those who were suffering.

ST. ATHANASIUS OF ALEXANDRIA (4TH C.)

272

Love and *then* what you will, do.

ST. AUGUSTINE OF HIPPO (5TH C.)

273

What is impossible to God? Not that which is difficult to his power, but that which is contrary to his nature.

ST. AMBROSE (4TH C.)

274

Rulers who prefer popular opinion to truth have as much power as robbers in the desert.

ST. JUSTIN MARTYR (2ND C.)

275

This is our Lord's will: that we trust him and search for him, enjoy him and delight in him, and comfort and strengthen ourselves, as by his help and grace we may, until such time as we see him face to face.

BL. JULIAN OF NORWICH (15TH C.)

276

In three different ways, woman can fulfill the mission of motherliness: in marriage, in the practice of a profession which values human development ... and under the veil as a spouse of Christ.

ST. EDITH STEIN (20TH C.)

277

Man is created to praise, reverence, and serve God our Lord, and by this means to save his soul. All other things on the face of the earth are created for man to help him fulfill the end for which he is created. From this it follows that man is to use these things to the extent that they will help him to attain his end. Likewise, he must rid himself of them in so far as they prevent him from attaining it.

ST. IGNATIUS LOYOLA (16TH C.)

278

The bread you store up belongs to the hungry; the cloak that lies in your chest belongs to the naked; the gold that you have hidden in the ground belongs to the poor.

ST. BASIL THE GREAT (4TH C.)

279

Divine Scripture is the feast of wisdom, and the single books are the various dishes.

ST. AMBROSE (4TH C.)

280

So now it's miracles they want from me. As if I didn't have enough to do already!

ST. PIUS X (20TH C.)

281

Know, most dearly beloved ... that courtesy is one of the properties of God, who gives his sun and rain to the just and the unjust by courtesy; and courtesy is the sister of charity, by which hatred is vanquished and love is cherished.

ST. FRANCIS OF ASSISI (13TH C.)

282

When our Lord sees pure souls coming eagerly to visit him in the Blessed Sacrament, he smiles on them. They come with that simplicity that pleases him so much.

ST. JOHN VIANNEY (19TH C.)

283

Out of gratitude and love for him, we should desire to be reckoned fools and glory in wearing his livery.

ST. IGNATIUS LOYOLA (16TH C.)

284

Since he is the Sun of Justice, he fittingly calls his disciples the light of the world. The reason for this is that through them, as through shining rays, he has poured out the light of the knowledge of himself upon the entire world.

ST. CHROMATIUS OF AQUILEIA (5TH C.)

285

O God, you seek those who hide from you, and hide from those who seek you!

ST. AUGUSTINE OF HIPPO (5TH C.)

286

When all the joys of heaven come flooding into a human heart how difficult it is for that heart, still in exile, to stand the strain of the impact without finding relief in tears.

ST. THÉRÈSE OF LISIEUX (19TH C.)

287

The Lord is loving unto man, and swift to pardon, but slow to punish. Let no man therefore despair of his own salvation.

ST. CYRIL OF JERUSALEM (4TH C.)

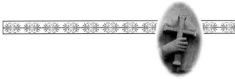

288

First learn to love yourself, and then you can love me.

ST. BERNARD OF CLAIRVAUX (12TH C.)

289

Life is given us that we may learn to die well, and we never think of it!
To die well we must live well.

ST. JOHN VIANNEY (19TH C.)

290

I see paradise has no gate, but whosoever will may enter therein, for God is all mercy and stands with open arms to admit us to his glory.

ST. CATHERINE OF GENOA (15TH C.)

291

Whoever entertains in his heart any trace of hatred for anyone, regardless of what the offense may have been, is a complete stranger to the love of God.

ST. MAXIMUS THE CONFESSOR (7TH C.)

292

A tree is shown by its fruits, and in the same way those who profess to belong to Christ will be seen by what they do.

ST. IGNATIUS LOYOLA (16TH C.)

293

He said not, "Thou shalt not be tempested, thou shalt not be travailed, thou shalt not be afflicted," but he said, "Thou shalt not be overcome."

BL. JULIAN OF NORWICH (15TH C.)

294

He causes his prayers to be of more avail to himself, who offers them also for others.

ST. GREGORY I (6TH C.)

295

To me, it has always seemed strange that God could restrict his mercy to the boundaries of the visible Church. God is truth, and whoever seeks the truth is seeking God, whether he knows it or not.

ST. EDITH STEIN (20TH C.)

296

Trust the past to the mercy of God, and the present to his love, and the future to his providence.

ST. AUGUSTINE OF HIPPO (5TH C.)

297

O God make us children of quietness, and heirs of peace.

ST. CLEMENT OF ALEXANDRIA (3RD C.)

298

Christ moves among the pots and pans.

ST. TERESA OF AVILA (16TH C.)

299

To him who still remains in this world no repentance is too late. The approach to God's mercy is open, and the access is easy to those who seek and apprehend the truth.

ST. CYPRIAN (3RD C.)

300

The air is in the sunshine and the sunshine in the air. So likewise is
God in the being of the soul....

BL. JOHN VAN RUYSBROECK (14TH C.)

301

Tolerance is the bond of all friendship, and unites people in heart and
opinion and action, not only with each other, but in unity with our
Lord, so that they may really be at peace.

ST. VINCENT DE PAUL (17TH C.)

302

If you want God to hear your prayers, hear the voice of the poor.

ST. THOMAS OF VILLANOVA (16TH. C)

303

Christ is rich, who will maintain you. He is a King, who will provide for you. He ia s sumptuous entertainer, who will feast you. He is beautiful, who will give in abundance all that can make you happy.

ST. EDMUND CAMPION (16TH C.)

304

Prayer, fasting, and mercy—through these three things faith stands firm, devotion abides and virtue endures. What prayer knocks for on the door, fasting successfully begs and mercy receives. These three give life to one another. For fasting is the soul of prayer. And mercy, the life of fasting.

ST. PETER CHRYSOLOGUS (5TH C.)

305

Farewell, my dear child, and pray for me and I shall for you and all your friends that we may merrily meet in heaven.

ST. THOMAS MORE (16TH C.)

306

Silence is a gift of God, to let us speak more intimately with God.

ST. VINCENT PALLOTTI (19TH C.)

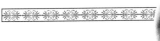

307

Make sickness itself a prayer.

St. Francis de Sales (17th c.)

308

The Father uttered one Word; that Word is his Son, and he utters him forever in everlasting silence; and in silence the soul has to hear it.

St. John of the Cross (16th c.)

309

Through obedience and discipline and training, we, who are created and contingent, grow into the image and likeness of the eternal God.

ST. IRENAEUS (2ND C.)

310

When you are our strength, it is strength indeed, but when our strength is our own it is only weakness.

ST. AUGUSTINE OF HIPPO (5TH C.)

311

Full lovingly does our Lord hold us when it seems to us we are nearly forsaken and cast away because of our sin—and deservedly so.

BL. JULIAN OF NORWICH (15TH C.)

312

Suffering is the very best gift he has to give us. He gives it only to his chosen friends.

ST. THÉRÈSE OF LISIEUX (19TH C.)

313

The Lord's Day is so called because on that day, the joy of our Lord's resurrection is celebrated.... [I]t was declared by the Christians in honor of the Lord's resurrection, and the celebration began from that time.

ST. ISIDORE OF SEVILLE (7TH C.)

314

One act of thanksgiving when things go wrong with us is worth a thousand thanks when things are agreeable to our inclination.

ST. JOHN OF AVILA (16TH C.)

315

Occupy your minds with good thoughts, or the enemy will fill them with bad ones: unoccupied they cannot be.

ST. THOMAS MORE (16TH C.)

316

God is faithful, and if we serve him faithfully, he will provide for our needs.

ST. RICHARD OF CHICHESTER (13TH C.)

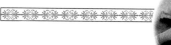

317

It is no use walking anywhere to preach unless we preach as we walk.

ST. FRANCIS OF ASSISI (13TH C.)

318

Consider seriously how quickly people change, and how little trust is to be had in them; and cleave fast unto God, who changes not.

ST. TERESA OF AVILA (16TH C.)

319

Sorrow can be alleviated by good sleep, a bath, and a glass of wine.

ST. THOMAS AQUINAS (13TH C.)

320

He is not wise to me who is wise in words only, but he who is wise in deeds.

ST. GREGORY I (6TH C.)

321

You will find something far greater in the woods than you will in books. Stones and trees will teach you what you can never learn from masters.

ST. BERNARD OF CLAIRVAUX (12TH C.)

322

Our words are a faithful index of the state of our souls.

ST. FRANCIS DE SALES (17TH C.)

323

I'm convinced that whenever God calls someone [in death], it's not for the sake of that person alone, and that, every time he does call anyone, he's lavish in offering proofs of his love.

ST. EDITH STEIN (20TH C.)

324

A man who governs his passions is master of the world. We must either rule them, or be ruled by them. It is better to be the hammer than the anvil.

ST. DOMINIC (13TH C.)

325

If the actions of our neighbors have a hundred sides, we ought always to look at them on the best side. When an action is blameworthy, we should strive to see the good intentions back of it.

St. Theresa Margaret of the Sacred Heart (18th c.)

326

An egg given during life for love of God is more profitable for eternity than a cathedral full of gold given after death.

St. Albert the Great (13th c.)

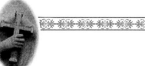

327

Imagine yourselves to be spiritual beggars in the presence of God and his saints. You should go round from saint to saint, imploring an alms with the same real earnestness with which the poor beg.

ST. PHILIP NERI (16TH C.)

328

A sinner who repents learns to be prudent. He is like an ass that, once he has fallen, afterwards looks more carefully where he sets his foot. For fear of punishment he takes care not to fall into those sins again, or into any others.

ST. BERNARDINO OF SIENA (15TH C.)

329

The question alone important, the solution of which depends upon how I have spent my life, is the state of my soul at the moment of death. Infinite misery or infinite happiness! There is no half and half, either one or the other.

BL. KATHARINE DREXEL (20TH C.)

330

Even if all hell's devils came against you to tempt you, you won't sin unless you *want* to—provided that you trust not in your own powers, but in the assistance of God. He doesn't refuse help to those who ask it with a lively faith.

ST. LEONARD OF PORT MAURICE (18TH C.)

331

Help me, O Lord, that my tongue may be merciful, so that I should never speak negatively of my neighbor, but have a word of comfort and forgiveness for all.

BL. FAUSTINA KOWALSKA (20TH C.)

332

O Lord Jesus, I surrender to you all my will. Let me be your lute. Touch any string you please. Always and forever let me make music in perfect harmony with your own. Yes, Lord, with no ifs, ands or buts, let your will be done in me.

ST. JANE DE CHANTAL (17TH C.)

333

The Church is like a great ship being pounded by the waves of life's different stresses. Our duty is not to abandon ship, but to keep her on her course.

St. Boniface (8th c.)

334

I include Ludwig [her husband] in my love for God, and I hope that God, who sanctified marriage, will grant us an eternal life.

St. Elizabeth of Hungary (13th c.)

335

The good Lord wants us happy. His hands are full of graces. He seeks someone to give it to, and, ah, no one wants it.

ST. JOHN VIANNEY (19TH C.)

336

If my Father was on one side and the devil on the other, and if the devil's cause were just, then the devil would get his due.

ST. THOMAS MORE (16TH C.)

337

What good would it do me if I saw myself in possession of everlasting life, but your people were dying?

ST. CATHERINE OF SIENA (14TH C.)

338

Happy the one who bears his neighbor with all his shortcomings as he wishes to be borne by him in his own weakness.

ST. FRANCIS OF ASSISI (13TH C.)

339

Everything our good Lord makes us to pray for, he has ordained that we should have since before time began.

BL. JULIAN OF NORWICH (15TH C.)

340

It is an old custom of the servants of God to have some little prayers ready and to be frequently darting them up to heaven during the day, lifting their minds to God.

ST. PHILIP NERI (16TH C.)

341

The servants of Christ are protected by invisible, rather than visible, beings. But if these guard you, they do so because they have been summoned by your prayers.

ST. AMBROSE (4TH C.)

342

For the sake of each of us he laid down his life—worth no less than the universe. He demands of us in return our lives for the sake of each other.

ST. CLEMENT OF ALEXANDRIA (3RD C.)

343

The house of mourning teaches charity and wisdom.

ST. JOHN CHRYSOSTOM (5TH C.)

344

Charity is that with which no one is lost, and without which no one is saved.

ST. ROBERT BELLARMINE (17TH C.)

345

A Christian is not his own master, since all his time belongs to God.

ST. IGNATIUS OF ANTIOCH (2ND C.)

346

It is better to confess your sins than to harden your heart.

ST. CLEMENT I (1ST C.)

347

In sorrow and suffering, go straight to God with confidence, and you will be strengthened, enlightened, and instructed.

ST. JOHN OF THE CROSS (16TH C.)

348

We cannot help conforming ourselves to what we love.

ST. FRANCIS DE SALES (17TH C.)

349

If up to now, a person has been more or less contented with himself,
the time for that is over.

ST. EDITH STEIN (20TH C.)

350

No matter how enlightened one may be through natural and acquired
knowledge, he cannot enter into himself to delight in the Lord unless
Christ be his mediator.

ST. BONAVENTURE (13TH C.)

351

God is not a deceiver, that he should offer to support us, and then, when we lean upon him, should slip away from us.

St. Augustine of Hippo (5th c.)

352

For we are by nature afraid of death and of the dissolution of the body; but there is this most startling fact, that the one who has put on the faith of the cross despises even what is naturally fearful, and for Christ's sake is not afraid of death.

St. Athanasius (4th c.)

353

When we die we shall come to God knowing ourselves clearly, having God wholly. We shall be enfolded in God for ever, seeing him truly, feeling him fully, hearing him spiritually, smelling him delectably, and tasting him sweetly.

BL. JULIAN OF NORWICH (15TH C.)

354

What greater work is there than training the mind and forming the habits of the young?

ST. JOHN CHRYSOSTOM (5TH C.)

355

Without the support of faith, good works cannot stand.

ST. AMBROSE (4TH C.)

356

The most Blessed Sacrament is Christ made visible. The poor sick person is Christ again made visible.

ST. GERARD MAJELLA (18TH C.)

357

We must know that God regards our purity of heart and tears of compunction, not our many words. Prayer should therefore be short and pure.

ST. BENEDICT OF NURSIA (6TH C.)

358

Everyone cannot become a genius, but the path of holiness is open to all.

ST. MAXIMILIAN KOLBE (20TH C.)

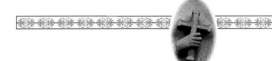

359

He doesn't call the people who are worthy of it; no, just the people it pleases him to call.

St. Thérèse of Lisieux (19th c.)

360

This morning my soul is greater than the world since it possesses you, you whom heaven and earth do not contain.

St. Margaret of Cortona (13th c.)

361

I worry until midnight and from then on I let God worry.

BL. LOUIS GUANELLA (19TH C.)

362

I have what God wished me to have, and I want no more.

ST. GERMAINE COUSIN (16TH C.)

363

It is a bigger miracle to be patient and refrain from anger than it is to control the demons which fly through the air.

ST. JOHN CASSIAN (5TH C.)

364

I see God in the work of his hands and the marks of his love in every visible thing, and it sometimes happens that I am seized by a supreme joy which is above all other joys.

BL. TITUS BRANDSMA (20TH C.)

365

These Nazis will not kill our souls, since we prisoners certainly distinguish ourselves quite definitely from our tormentors; they will not be able to deprive us of the dignity of our Catholic belief. We will not give up. And when we die, then we die pure and peaceful, resigned to God in our hearts.

ST. MAXIMILIAN KOLBE (20TH C.)

366

There is no other Lord beside him whom I have seen. Him I worship and serve, and to him I will cling, though I should suffer a thousand deaths.

ST. GENESIUS THE ACTOR (2ND C.)